Animals of North America For Kids Amazing Animal Books for Young Readers

by John Davidson

Read More Amazing Animal Books

Table of Contents

Introduction

What Fun Are The Animals Of North America?

There are several animals that are native to the great upper part of the Western hemi-shire. Yes, of course I am speaking of the land mass known as North America. When looking at all the animals that we have here now it can seem like they have been here forever, but that is not so. A lot of animals such as horses, pigs, goats, and cows came over to this country from Europe just like many of your families did a long, long time ago. There are some animals however that are native to this great country we call America.

One of our most feared furry friends is native to this great continent. Have you ever been camping? Well, if you have then these guys may have been a concern for you while you were resting up in that cozy tent. The brown Bear is a native North American mammal that can be found all over the west coast. These guys have a high temper but will usually leave you alone as long as you respect their space.

Have you ever heard noises coming from the attic? Well, guess what kids. It was in fact not a scary monster that has it in for little boys. The creature that was probably wrestling through your Attic was none other than the North American native raccoon. He was probably just hungry and looking for a snack? That's why we see them so often in our garbage. They don't care so much about germs like us Humans do.

Do you ever notice an Icky smell during a long car ride back home? Well, when you do it is probably none other than the North American Skunk. These guys are cute but don't let their adorable looks fool you, they can make you quite stinky if you get to close. When you see an animal with black and white fur it could be a skunk. It is always best to try and keep your distance!

Ever gotten hungry and had a quick snack at McDonald's? Well, did you know that the beef they used could either be from the European cow or it could be from an American Bison? Both are considered beef and can be sold as such.

I hope this has helped you see that many great critters come from this land. Make sure that you do the right thing by respecting their environment!

1. Large Mammals of Yellowstone

Yellowstone National Park stretches across Wyoming, and into parts of Idaho and Montana. It is home to many different types of animals and is a popular place to visit for anyone who loves nature.

The largest mammal found in Yellowstone is the bison. These vegetarian giants graze on the grass found all over the meadows, foothills, and high plateaus of the park. A male bison, called a bull, can weigh almost 2,000 pounds! Bison stand 6 feet tall, which is taller than the average person. Even though they are very large, Bison can run up to 30 miles per hour and are not afraid of defending their young.

Bison - © vanfan - Fotolia.com

The bear is another very large mammal found in Yellowstone. Both grizzly and black bears can be found wandering around the park. Bears love to eat the trout that are common in the streams of

Yellowstone. Black bears are the smaller of the two types of bears, reaching up to 300 pounds. Grizzly bears can get much bigger, with some males getting to 700 pounds or more!

Bighorn sheep are found throughout the mountains of Yellowstone. These sheep get their name from their large horns, which can weigh up to 30 pounds all by themselves. Only males grow large horns. Female sheep, called ewes, have much smaller horns. They graze on any grasses and shrubbery that they can find while they wander.

Yellowstone is also home to the mountain lion or cougar. The mountain lion is the largest cat found in the park. It has two smaller cousins, the lynx and the bobcat. Mountain lions were hunted in the past, making them a rare sight in Yellowstone today. There are only around 20 of these cats left in the park.

The gray wolf is another animal that has become rare in Yellowstone. In fact, because of hunting, they were almost completely gone. Scientists and nature conservationists have been working to help the gray wolf come back to Yellowstone by protecting the few remaining packs and even introducing a few new ones, brought in from areas where wolves are not as rare.

Elk, deer, and moose are all hoofed mammals you can find in Yellowstone. Elk are the most common, and almost everyone who visits Yellowstone will see a few wandering around. There are more than 30 thousand in the park, broken up into 7 or 8 large herds. Deer are also common, however moose are only found in a small section of the park.

There are many animals found in Yellowstone's over 3,000 square mile boundaries. Countless creatures have found a safe haven here, where they can be free to roam the wild like they did hundreds of years ago.

2. Bighorns

The bighorn sheep, known by their scientific name as Ovis canadensis, are also called mountain sheep. These hardy, climbing hoofed sheep are found in the western parts of North America, and are identified by large, dense curling horns and white spots on their bottoms. Both male and female have these horns. Males tend to have a bit larger horns than females. When measuring along the outer curvature of the horn, some researchers have found them to be over a yard long.

Bighorns like to eat sedge, herbs, grass, and shrubs. They belong to a group of animals known as ruminants, or herbivores, meaning that they only eat vegetation. Open, rocky terrain is their habitat of choice. A migratory mammal, the bighorn will travel seasonally between one and twenty miles, a broad spectrum but nonetheless this has been documented. Some of them weigh up to 300 pounds, but the average male size tends to be 210 pounds, with the average female size coming in at 155 pounds. At birth, lambs can weigh up to 11 pounds. Interestingly, bighorns segregate themselves based on their sex, living in groups ranging from two to twelve sheep. In ideal circumstances, the bighorn can live to be 20 years of age.

Scientists are convinced that, at one time, up to two million bighorns lived in the space from Canada down to Mexico. In the 1800s, they were driven to the brink of extinction. Dedicated conservationists have helped increase their number significantly, but they are not considered fully recovered from their near wipe out. Some subspecies are considered endangered, others just threatened. Either way, ongoing conservation programs continue to try and bolster the numbers of this fine creature. As where irresponsible hunting methods were once an issue, now livestock diseases are one of the main challenges facing conservationists trying to aid in the comeback of the bighorn.

Like many mammals right before mating season rituals can be quite violent, and bighorns are known for ramming their heads into each other. There are two layers of bone in the bighorn's skull, so injury is avoided.

Between the ages of three and four, bighorn ewes will bear their first offspring. After a gestation period lasting approximately six months, lambs are born in the springtime, and are weaned before the winter comes. (Weaning means they are no longer fed the mother's milk, and are introduced to solid food.) Sadly many lambs die due to malnutrition.

With literally countless bighorn conservation groups established throughout the western half of North America trying to do their bit, and with the help of generous donations, the bighorn sheep's future is not yet entirely stable but hopefully will be in the future. Otherwise the ecosystem, and ultimately humans will pay a high price for the bighorns extinction.

3. Coyotes

The Coyote is a member of the canine family. Also called the brush wolf, or prairie wolf, it is known in the scientific community as Canis latrans. We get the name coyote from an ancient Aztec word, coyote.

The mating season for coyotes lasts between January and March. The gestation period is very similar to wolves and dogs, lasting between 58 and 65 days. Litters usually yield between four and seven pups. Babies are born blind, but this begins to change after two weeks. By the time they are full grown, coyotes have fairly keen vision, hunting by sight on open plains. Pups are weaned around six weeks, and are fully grown between six and nine months.

Weighing in at between 20 to 50 pounds, the coyote stands approximately two feet at the shoulder and can achieve speeds of up to 40 miles per hour at full run. The coat of the coyote is coarse and hard, with varying darkish colors. Known mostly for its chorus of howls that can often be heard at night if you live near a pack, coyotes are found throughout North and Central America. Their lifespan can be as long as 21 years, but with the harsh conditions of day to day living in the wild, few make it that far. Most die around seven years of age. Often, premature death is brought on by various diseases mostly unique to canines, such as distemper and rabies. Another disease, called mange, causes hair to fall out. This in turn leaves the coyote vulnerable to cold exposure during the winter months, and often kills him.

Like the wolf, coyotes can cross breed with domestic dogs. Unlike certain canine species, coyotes are a far cry from being endangered. In North America, their numbers are higher now than they have ever been before. Rather than implementing conservation methods, culling measures are in place throughout many areas. Even where many coyotes are shot, the populations remain very healthy. Cattle and sheep farmers have to be particularly vigilant in culling, and even though many respect the coyote, they can really wreak havoc on a farmer's business. There have been many cases of attacks on humans by coyotes, including one fatality. They are so abundant, they are also dying in large numbers in road collisions. Keeping roads safer and ending the coyotes lives more humanely is one of the many benefits of culling.

The coyote is an opportunist and an excellent hunter. However, while mostly a carnivore or meat eater, the coyote is a confirmed omnivore, meaning he will eat meat or vegetation. Like wild dogs and wolves, coyotes often hunt The coyote is an opportunist, and an excellent hunter. However, while mostly a carnivore or meat eater, the coyote is a confirmed omnivore, meaning he will eat meat or vegetation. Like wild dogs and wolves, coyotes often hunt in packs, but sometimes in pairs. Both white-tailed deer and the snowshoe hair are on the coyote's menu, as is carrion, berries, and fruits. They kill deer by biting at the back legs over and over until the deer is grounded. Then they finalize the kill by biting down on the neck and choking the deer. Coyotes prefer to take the path of least resistance, and hence do most of their hunting in areas with little snow accumulation. This makes travel and mobility very easy. While a formidable predator, the coyote is not at the top of the food chain and will be preyed on by both large wolves and cougars.

It's safe to say that coyotes will be around for a long time to come, though too much culling could yield problems in the future if people are overzealous in killing them. Only time will tell how the coyote fairs in the future. But for now, he roams healthy and free as one of North Americas top predators.

4. Moose

The moose is one of nature's finest beasts. Strong and tall the moose is easy to spot with his dewlap (the little "goatee" hanging from his throat) and wide antlers. Known to scientists as Alces, the moose gets its English name from the word moosh, an Algonquian word meaning eater of bark.

The largest member of the deer family, moose are found in both North America and Eurasia. Moose can really vary in size, weighing up to 1,300 pounds in areas such as Siberia and Alaska, but only up to 770 pounds in states like Wyoming and northeast China.

While they look docile moose are good at defending themselves against attack from predators such as Grizzly bears and packs of wolves, sometimes even killing wolves in the course of their defense. While there have only ever been two documented cases of wolves killing a person, moose have killed many people, though this is nearly always only after being provoked. As fast runners, moose usually try an escape a confrontation rather than engage in one. The common result of such a chase is that pursuing predators will tire out and give up long before the moose runs out of energy. Moose are also adept swimmers, even able to dive underwater for up to fifty seconds. Though they might not win an Olympic medal for running or swimming, they deserve our admiration for their efficiency in these two areas despite looking somewhat clumsy.

Moose diets consists of conifers in the winter, and eat aquatic vegetation in the summer. They do not eat meat, sticking only to vegetation. Animals that only eat vegetation are known as herbivores.

The mating season comes during the month of September, and calves are born in June, a period lasting about 230 days. It is not uncommon for a moose to have twins. The mother is very protective when the calves are young, but she drives them away when they are old enough to go out on their own. Often Bulls, or male moose, will attract females with the scent of their urine during the mating season, or rut. They do this by urinating onto muddy parts of the ground, and then using their legs to splash the urine laced mud onto their undersides. Cows, or female moose, are a little less gross in the way they attract males, simply using their call.

Hunting almost wiped the moose out in the nineteenth century, but hunters got together and sought to regulate moose hunting to save the moose from extinction. This happened to many animal species around the nineteenth century, but many including the moose, responded well to efforts to restore them. Unfortunately, moose are again on the decline in North America with the reintroduction of a predator fauna. For this reason hunting continues to remain regulated, with most states issuing a hunting license on a lottery basis. This limits the amount of people that can get a license leaving adequate numbers of the moose population healthy and strong.

5. Wolves

The wolf. Also known as Canis lupus and the bane of the livestock farmer's life, this canine is actually a lot more closely related to the dog you have at home than you think. In fact, you can even breed a common dog with a wolf. The wolf is any of three species: the gray wolf or timber wolf which is the best known, the red wolf, and the Abyssinian wolf. Wolves were domesticated several thousand years ago, with breeding methods producing what we now know as the domesticated dog. Both the wolf and dog share the same amount of chromosomes, 78, distinguishing them from jackals and foxes who have less.

Wolves can actually run up to 37 miles per hour, and with large, powerful jaws, they are good at hunting. Despite their strength, wolves are not usually powerful enough to kill prey by themselves, which is why they hunt in packs. A male may be about 6 and a half feet long, and weighing up to 100 pounds, and standing about two and a half feet tall at its shoulder. Weight can be much more or much less depending on the area the wolf lives in, and female wolves are about 20% smaller than their male counterparts. The largest wolves are found in Alaska, west-central Canada, and northern Asia. The smallest are usually found in India and the Middle East.

The coloring of a wolf's fur is usually gray, but runs through a spectrum including reddish, brown, white, and black. The lightest of these color patterns are found in the arctic regions.

Canada has the largest population of wolves on the planet, followed closely by the US states of Alaska and Minnesota. Wolves can also be found in Wisconsin, Idaho and Michigan. Wolves are protected in Canada and the United States, as they were pushed the brink of extinction in the nineteenth and twentieth centuries. People mistakenly thought that wolves were dangerous to people, but in fact there have only been two recorded cases of wolves killing humans, the last of which happened in 2010. Really, the only justified killing of wolves since they are not hunted for sport or food, is when a cattle rancher must take action to protect his heard from hungry wolves.

Today, wolves have made a good comeback in North America. Traditionally a pack animal, wolf packs can include up to 24 wolves at a time, but packs numbering between six and ten are most common. A system of government, along with a sort of camaraderie is evident in these packs. Wolf packs cover territories ranging between 30 to 1,200 square miles. The breeding season occurs between the months of February and April. Litters consist of about five pups after a very brief gestation period of just 60 days, and all members of the pack care for baby wolves. Their lifespan is about 12 years, but starvation, disease and injury often kill them before that age.

6. Cougars

Cougars are also called Mountain Lions. They are also called pumas and panthers. They live in North and South America and can adapt to a lot of climates, however, most of the cougars in the mid-west and eastern United States have been killed. So today, cougars mostly live in the Western part of the United States and Canada, in the Rocky Mountains, and also in many parts of South America.

The cougar will not roar like a lion does, but it is still and excellent hunter. The cougar likes to live in areas where there is a lot of thick brush and rocks because it uses these to hide from its prey when it is hunting.

The cougar is a meat eater, it does not eat plants. In North America, it often eats deer, but it will also eat smaller animals like squirrels or raccoons. It is also known to eat even larger animals, like cattle. Cougars hunt and live alone, they are a solitary animal.

Cougars are very fast and agile. They are the 4th largest of the large cats. Adult male cougars are about eight feet long on average, from the nose to the tail. The average male cougar weighs 140 pounds, but larger males can weigh as much as 220 pounds. The average female cougar weighs about 95 pounds.

7. Elk

The elk, one of nature's forest kings, majestic, and admired by man for thousands of years. What is an elk though? Basically, an elk is the largest type of red deer. Known to scientists as Cervus elaphus canadensis, the English word elk comes from an old German word meaning hart or stag. The Shawnee tribe know elk as the white deer, or wapiti.

This giant can be found in both Central Asia and North America. How much an elk will weigh depends much on where it lives. In southern California, elk average about 240 pounds, while in Alberta they can reach 840 pound significant difference in weight, but also a significant distance apart.

To protect themselves from predators, the elk will stay in a group or herd, and they prefer grazing on open plains. The gestation period of the elk lasts 255 days, or about eight months. (Gestation means the time it take for the baby to grow until it is ready to be born.) All male elk have a high-pitched bugling call. They can be heard making this call during the rut, or mating season. Their call is designed to carry long distances and reach other elk far away in open landscapes. Sometimes, females will make a bugling call as the male does. Elk do not like deserts, tundra, or boreal forests.

Male elk keep their antlers about 185 days before shedding them. That is about as many days as you are in school. Sometimes, these antlers are cut off the elk before they are ready to be shed and are used in folk medicines by native peoples in Asia. The coats of elks are light tan, light brown body color, but in winter they get darker around their necks, which really makes them stand out.

Archaeologists think the elk population grew so much because European diseases wiped out so many Native Americans, which was one of the elk's main predators. Elk were prized by natives more for their hide and their symbolism than for their meat. Hunters today still admire and respect the elk for the forest king it is. In the nineteenth century, hunting was not as regulated as it is today, and the elk was hunted almost to extinction. Hunters decided to fix this problem by forming conservation groups, and strictly limiting the amount of elk people could hunt. They successfully reversed the problem, and now elk are abundant in number once again. It is important that some elk are hunted for the health of the herd, but strict regulation on how that is done will hopefully keep the elk hopping around for years to come so all can enjoy this beautiful creature's presence in the outdoors.

8. Pronghorn

The American antelope or pronghorn is a unique creature in more ways than one. Known to scientists as Antilocapra americana, this hoofed mammal is found in North America. One thing that makes it so unique, is that it is the only living member of the ruminant family of Antilocapridae. It is also the only animal in the world that has branching horns that are shed on a yearly basis, and both male and female have horns. Male horns are longer than female horns and branch up into two prongs. Males shed the horns in October, which is after the pronghorn's mating season. During the winter, the horns begin to grow back, and are fully grown by the time territorial contesting begins in the spring. Reddish brown and white in coloring, he sports a dark mane. Contrary to what the name suggests, pronghorn are not closely related to antelope.

The mating season for the pronghorn is quite brief, beginning in late summer and lasting to early autumn. Males make good use of summer vegetation for nutrition and energy, which is depleted through the mating rituals. The gestation period, or time it takes the baby to grow before birth, is very long, lasting 250 days.

Though six embryos are usually fertilized, only two ever survive to birth. So like the moose, twin births are common among pronghorns.

The pronghorn is actually quite small, standing about one yard high at the shoulder, and weighing a mere 90 pounds. Some females weight even less than this. But where they lack in size, the excel in speed. Did you know that some antelope can reach speeds of up to 40 miles per hour? As if that's not impressive enough, the pronghorn can leap over 20 feet in a single bound! Also interestingly, the pronghorn has eyes as big as an elephant's and have excellent eyesight, being able to spot predators up to half a mile away. They communicate by raising up their bottoms, which are easily spotted by each other due to their good eyesight. Open plains, grassland, fields, brush and desert are the favored habitats of the pronghorn, forming large herds by winter. They are found in the band from Alberta to northern Mexico. Like many game animals, pronghorn were nearly wiped out due to irresponsible hunting practices in the nineteenth century. But pronghorns have returned in great numbers thanks to responsible hunters and devoted conservationists.

9. Grizzly Bears

The grizzly bear is one of the most beautiful and popular mammals at Yellowstone, but also one of the more dangerous. While they look lovable and like a friendly Teddy bear, you should be careful around them.

The grizzly bear is found throughout the western parts of North America, including Yellowstone. They are called grizzly bears because of gray hairs you can see in their fur coat.

Grizzly bears are very big. A female can way over 400 pounds and a male can weight almost 800 pounds in some cases. And, they can stand as tall as seven foot.

Grizzly bears are omnivores. That means they eat both plants and meat. One of their favorite things to eat is fish. They like to catch fish in streams and rivers and like salmon, trout and bass. They will also eat other animals like moose and deer. They also will eat pine nuts, berries, grass and will eat meat from animals that have died or been killed by other animals. In Yellowstone it has been found that they eat miller moths as well.

Grizzly bears eat a bunch of food to get ready for their winter hibernation. In fact, they can gain up to 400 pounds to get ready. Then when a big snowstorm comes they will enter their den and go into hibernation.

Grizzly bears are one of the more aggressive breeds of bears. Since they are so big they cannot escape danger as easily as smaller bears by running or climbing trees. So, they are more likely to attack when they feel threatened. A mother bear protecting her cubs are even more likely to attack if they feel threatened.

Grizzly bears do not usually attack or hunt people. In fact they usually try to avoid them. But, there are exceptions to this. If a bear is surprised, or feels their babies may be in danger they may attack.

Grizzly bears also like to scavenge for food. They have been known to come into camps and take food when no one is there, or even if people are there. A smart way to avoid that is to hang food and garbage above the ground where they can not reach it.

Grizzly bears are interesting and fun mammals to learn about. But, they should not be mistaken for harmless animals. They can be dangerous if you are not careful when around them. Hopefully, you have learned some things to understand them better.

10. Black Bears

The Black Bear is a native of North America. That means he lives in Canada and the United States of America. But there is also an Asiatic Black Bear which originates, as the name would suggest, in Asia. The Asiatic Black Bear is closely related to the Sun Bear.

The Asiatic Black Bear has a white crescent moon mark on its chest. But this type of marking is only found on about a quarter of North American Black Bears.

The Black Bear is a medium size bear, much smaller than his huge cousin the Grizzly Bear.

Black Bears, like people, are omnivores, which means that they eat both meat and vegetables. What they eat will depend on the weather and where they are. Basically if a bear is hungry enough he will eat anything.

Like all bears, the Black Bear will hibernate in winter. When they emerge from hibernation they will immediately look for food. Often they will eat dead animals that they find which have been killed by the winter conditions. They will also prey on the new born young of other animals.

They will also eat the spring shoots of many plants including grasses, trees and shrubs. In the summer they will move on to the fruit which becomes available. This is mainly made up of forest berries.

In autumn eating is the Black Bears full time job, as be has to stock up for the long winter hibernation. At this time of year they will eat acorns, pine nuts and hazelnuts. They will even steal the stored nuts hidden by squirrels. Of course any bears that live close to areas populated by humans will take advantage of the food sources that they provide. They will raid garbage, eat birdseed left out for wild birds and raid any agricultural stocks they can get into. Not forgetting of course honey, both from wild bees and honey farms.

Bears of course live in wooded areas and make use of the trees as a food source and to provide some shelter. They also use trees as a form of communication with other bears, by marking them with their claws and teeth. So maybe bears were the first creatures to create graffiti.

The Black Bear is doing very well in terms of survival. While many other types of bear are on the endangered list, there are estimated to be more than twice as many black bears than all of the other bear types combined. But they do struggle a little with habitat, because of all the forests that have been felled. So they are now found less widely than in years gone by.

11. Bison or Buffalo

The animal that most people in North America and many other places refer to as a Buffalo is in fact really a Bison. Buffalo are actually found in Africa and Asia and look quite different to the Buffalo that most of us know.

The Bison is a very distinctive looking animal with its woolly fur collar, the hump over its front legs and its thick coat which grows even thicker in winter to protect them from the cold conditions in North America. The Buffalo, living in Africa, of course does not need a thick coat of fur, as it is much warmer where they live.

The Bison also has short sharp horns which it uses for defense from predators like wolves and to fight with other Bison, usually for a mate. The African Buffalo has much longer horns, they are not as sharp, but they are basically used for the same purposes.

Bison can be very aggressive, if they feel threatened and will use their horns to attack. Whereas Buffalo are much more peaceful and they are even domesticated and used to help farmers pulling carts and plowing in much the same way as a horse or donkey.

Because of the harsh conditions in which they live Bison to usually only live into their teens, but Buffalo, living in much milder climates where food is much more readily available, can often live to twenty five or thirty years.

Most Buffalo are domesticated and either used as a beast of burden or bred for their meat and even milk. Bison have never been domesticated but have been reared for their meat.

There are only estimated to be around 420,000 Bison in the world with the vast majority of those being commercially bred to supply the meat trade. But Buffalo spread across Africa and Asia could number as many as one hundred and fifty million.

The Bison is the largest land animal in North America and a fully grown Bison could be as much as two hundred kilos or five hundred pounds, heavier than a fully grown Buffalo. But in their native lands Buffalo are dwarfed by animals such as Elephants, Rhinoceros and Hippopotamus for the title of the largest animal in their regions.

So if you are in North America, remember the next time that you see a Buffalo he is really a Bison and you may have to go to another country, or at least a Zoo to see a real Buffalo.

12. Skunks

The nasty smelling spray of a skunk remains legendary as a powerful deterrent against predators. The spray is actually an oily liquid substance produced in anal glands that reside under the skunk's large bushy tail. To deliver the "scent bomb" the furry creature turns its backside on the predator and blasts the foul misty oil. In fact, the oil can spray upwards of three meters (10 feet).

While the oily spray from the skunk does no actual damage to any of the skunk's victims, it provides a high level of discomfort that can linger for days on end. Even the most reliable method for removing the odor tends to be only minimally effective. The spray works to be a powerful defensive technique. Because of that, most predators provide skunks ample breathing room unless no other obvious food source is available.

Skunk Varieties

There are actually different varieties of skunks that vary in size. Most individuals are aware of the variety that never grows larger than a typical house cat. However, there are varieties of skunks with spots, swirl patterns and the most recognized striped variety. All of them share the intense deep black and stark white fur that provides easy identification to alert any predator that a potential pungent odor could be there as with any wrong movement.

Making a Home

Skunks tend to find homes underground and burrowed areas that have been built by other animal species. However, they also take up living quarters in abandoned buildings and hollowed out logs. During the colder months, skunks may become dormant (deep sleep) in their chosen domicile for weeks at a time. During their annual February breeding season, the female skunk births litters that contain 2 to 10 young every year. Gestation time for skunks is proximally 7 to 10 weeks, with the newborns arriving in May.

Eating Time

Skunks tend to be very opportunistic eaters that enjoy a variety of different types of food in their diet. All skunks tend to eat at night (nocturnal foragers) and enjoy worms, larva, insects, reptiles, eggs, fish, small mammals, plants, vegetables and fruit. Nearly every skunk in the world is indigenous to North, Central and South America. However, one exception to the American variety of skunks is the Asian Stink Badger, a close sibling in the skunk family.

Interesting Facts

While skunks have many predators, through their own predatory actions they often attack a beehive to enjoy the honey. They tend to live approximately 3 years unless domesticated, where they tend to live 10 years or more. The short legs on skunks are highly developed with claws that are used primarily for digging. They move slowly but have the ability to run nearly 10 miles an hour when necessary.

All varieties of skunks have an excellent sense of smell, nearly perfect hearing, and extremely poor vision. Because of that, baby skunks tend to stay close to the mother until late fall.

Skunks do not usually become aggressive around humans. However, they can carry rabies and should be avoided if not a domesticated pet.

13. Raccoons

Raccoons are common in North America and they look quite comical with those black bands around their eyes. In fact this may help them to reduce glare in the night as well as enhancing its night vision. This creature has a dense grayish brown coat which helps to keep him warm in the cold weather. There are also five and even up to eight light and dark rings around its tail.

If you see a raccoon run or walk, they often appear hunched over. This is because their hind legs and longer than their front ones. The tones on their front paws and amazingly dexterous which means they can grasp all sorts of objects, not just food. They can often pry open a well closed garbage bin and even open doorknobs, latches on doors or jars.

You can find raccoons all over the United States and Canada, except for places like Utah, Nevada and Arizona and parts of the Rock Mountains. They originally came from the Tropics but over time they migrated to the north. They are usually nocturnal. They adapt to all sorts of environments but they are no strangers to cities where they are found all over the place as there is an abundance of food that we humans discard and generally no real predators.

The raccoon is an omnivore so everything is considered food. They happily eat fruits, berries, nuts as well as small rodents, frogs and insects. They live on land but are also good swimmers and can happily stay in the water for hours at a time.

The female produces between two or five babies (called kits) usually in the spring. The male only participates in mating and leaves the care of the babies solely to the mother. Even when they are newly born, they already have their black masks. They stay in their nest up to ten weeks but they will only leave their mother when they are around 13 or 14 months old.

Raccoons are often considered pets in towns and cities. They steal around in the garbage, often knocking it over and leaving a mess. Also, if they can they will go through the chimney opening into the attic, particularly to nest and will only vacate this space when their babies are ready to be more independent.

They can live up to twenty years in captivity but only about two or three in the wild. In urban environments they are often killed by vehicles or they succumb to disease or infection. They can be carriers of rabies.

14. Chipmunks

Chipmunks are small rodents similar in appearance to squirrels,, although considerably smaller. Unlike the squirrel, they are striped. They are fairly sociable animals and very rather irresistible. But, cute as they are, you would do well to resist the temptation to feed them or get too close to them. They are, after all, wild animals and a bite by a chipmunk could invite all manner of complications, including rabies.

Chipmunks are common to certain areas of North America. They have also been called striped squirrels, as well as ground squirrels, timber tigers and chippers or munks. Their name comes from an Ottawa (a Native American tribe) Indian word, "jidmoonh, which means "red squirrel." Their diet consists of nuts, seeds and fruit, as well as certain vegetation.

Chipmunks are gatherers. They take refuge in their tunnels during the cold months of winter. The Eastern chipmunk hibernates while the Western variety simply bides its time until warmer weather arrives. In preparation for this long, dormant season they instinctively stockpile stashes of nuts and seeds to live on until spring. Generally, that is the time they come back out and begin procreating, although the Eastern Chipmunks breed during both spring and summer, while the Western variety mates only once a year.

We have small creatures such as chipmunks to thank for perpetuating our forests. While they are busying themselves gathering their seeds and nuts, they are inadvertently distributing some of those seeds to new areas where they begin new growth. They are responsible for this same kind of disbursements when it comes to fungi and spores that produce mushrooms and, in some locations, truffles. Thus these little creatures do far more for the ecology than just sit around looking adorable, although they are pretty good at that as well!

Chipmunks are also a source of food for other mammals and larger birds such as hawks and owls. But even as they cautiously avoid becoming some predatory bird's next meal, they are themselves preying on the eggs of other birds. Bluebirds have been known to gang up on a chipmunk who has an eye on one of their nests. It is the law of nature in action.

If you do not have the good fortune of living in an area that has a chipmunk population, you are really missing out. Some zoos have created very natural habitats for chipmunks, although in captivity they tend to sleep up to 15 hours daily.

15. Prairie Dogs

Have you heard of prairie dogs? What is interesting is that prairie dogs are actually not dogs at all. They are burrowing rodents that are found in North America. You have probably seen one before it you have ever been in the grasslands of Utah. There are actually five different species of this animal, some of which are related to some of the ground squirrels that you see. Although they are found prominently in the United States, they are also located throughout northern Mexico in the Sonora, Chihuahua, and northern Coahuila areas. These natural herbivores make a sound that is very similar to a dog's bark, hence leading to the name that they have today.

Many people actually have prairie dogs as pets. Although you would assume that this type of animal would not be sociable toward humans, this is actually contrary to what occurs. As long as you have a prairie dog at an early age, they will bond very easily with humans, very similar to canines and cats. If they do become domesticated, you must still remember that they are wild animals, and that their diet needs to be very similar to what they would eat in nature. Different types of grass should be provided, along with rabbit pellets in order to augment their diet to help them stay healthy.

Prairie dogs actually do not get that large. Since they are rodents, there are usually limited to about 15 inches in length which will include their very short tail. They might weigh as much as 3 pounds and they have a tendency to stand upright in a bipedal fashion. It is very natural for them to burrow underground, with many burrows reaching a length of over 30 feet in length, descending over 10 feet beneath the ground. They will usually have multiple holes leading into the area below, usually marked by small mounds. By having multiple holes, not only do they have many different ways to escape predators, but it also allows them to have multiple sources of fresh air in case one of the holes is accidentally shut.

In conclusion, prairie dogs are astounding creatures that have been documented even as far back as the Lewis and Clark journals. If you would like to see one, and you live in the grassland areas of the United States, Canada, or Mexico, you should be able to see one, if not hear one, on occasion, an event that you won't soon forget.

16. Roadrunners

One of the most interesting species of birds is the roadrunner. It is a bird that is black and brown in color, very slender, with a very distinctive head crest. It has a dark oversized bill, very long legs, and has a tail with white tips on three of its outer tail feathers. Another unique feature is the blank patch of skin which is located behind each of its eyes which is red or blue in color. It is a terrestrial bird that can actually fly, yet it spends most of its life running along the ground. If you are lucky enough to see one fly, you will see that the wings are rounded and short, revealing a white crescent created by feathers on its wings. It is a member of the cuckoo family, having only two toes in back and two in the front, something that is technically called zygodactyl feet. Although it can escape predators by flying away, it is more likely to see a roadrunner running at speeds of almost 20 miles an hour to escape any danger.

If you live in the desert regions of the United States, and to even out as far as Missouri or Western Louisiana, you have probably seen these birds running around. Although most of birds tend to focus only on worms and insects for food, roadrunners will eat crickets, lizards, bird eggs, snakes, scorpions and even hummingbirds. It may be because of their excessive running that they need an extremely high protein diet in order to survive. Many people will put up hummingbird feeders, not to feed the hummingbirds, but to attract roadrunners if they are in the area.

There are many other interesting aspects of the roadrunner including the fact that it will secrete excess salt that is in its bloodstream through salt glands located at the front of its eyes. As long as roadrunners eat enough food with high water content, it can actually live for quite some time without drinking water. Roadrunners are also able to expose the skin on their back by fluffing their feathers, allowing them to absorb heat from the sun so that they can survive cold desert nights. Also, despite the popularity of the roadrunner cartoon, it does not make a "beep beep" noise, but something more similar to a cooing sound. If you live in the southwestern United States, northern Mexico, or if you ever visit Baja California, you should be able to see a roadrunner passing by.

17. Bald Eagles

The American bald eagle is the national birth of North America. Surprisingly it is not bald at all! This is because the world bald actually meant white and this huge bird of prey has a signature white head and neck with a blackish brown body and a white tail. Their beak is sharp and scary looking and at the tip it has a hook which is used for tearing flesh and it can also be used as a weapon. Their talons kill their prey with their talons and they can pen and close them at will.

As with many birds, the male is slightly smaller than the female whose body length can vary from 35 to 37 inches and their wingspan can reach 90 inches. The male is a much smaller 30 to 34 inches but still has a wingspan up to 85 inches. An average bald eagle weighs in at ten to fourteen pounds. They can lift up to about four pounds. While these amazing birds can live up to thirty years, on average their lifespan is around fifteen to twenty.

While half of the bald eagles in the world live in Alaska (35,000) and 20,000 in British Columbia, Canada, the rest can be found everywhere in North America, including northern Mexico. They love the North West coast of America because this is where they can feast on salmon. Fish, alive or dead are an important source of food for all bald eagles. For this reason they are often found where there is water – either along the Pacific coast or on lakes or rivers. They are carrion birds and will feed on creatures that are dead or decaying.

Scientifically speaking bald eagles are actually a sea or fish eagle and there are two subspecies. The southern bald eagle resides in places which are south of 40 degrees latitude. This means Texas, Southern California, the Gulf States as well as South Carolina and Florida. Bald eagles that can be found north of this latitude are the northern bald eagles and they generally veer towards the North West. This eagle is a little bit bigger than its southern counterpart.

Their eyesight is sharp and at least four times as much as a person with perfect vision. Their eyes are quite large – almost as large as ours. They have a high pitched cry even though they have no vocal cords. Their sound is produced in a bony chamber called a syrinx. They use their shrill calls to warn other eagles or predators that this area they are calling from is defended by them.

18. California Sea Lions

Although the California Sea Lion is named for a State that they like to visit, they can, in actuality, be found anywhere from British Columbia to Mexico. They like to breed on sparsely populated islands off of the coast, and often frequent the Galapogos Islands.

California Sea Lion pups are typically born in the beginning of the summer season and they weigh approximately twenty pounds at birth. California Sea Lions are nursed for at least the first six months of their lives but have been shown to nurse for up to a full-year period. Sea Lion mothers are able to recognize their young by smell and by distinctive vocalizations. Pups learn to recognize their mother's call at a very young age. Adult males dutifully patrol breeding territory, and look to breed within weeks of a mother giving birth to her latest offspring.

California Sea Lions, like other species, are incredibly social animals. They spend lots of time together for safety as well as more social aspect. Groups of California Sea Lions can often be found resting on the shore or floating on the surface of the ocean in self-fashioned raft. Interestingly, spectators can often watch these sea lions apparently "surfing" on breaking waves, and they often jump in and out of the water in an effort to swim faster and more cohesively.

The California Sea Lion diet consists of whatever happens to be available in large supply. They eat everything from octopus to small sharks. They also take their own place on the food chain, and are often the favorite food of both great white sharks and Orca whales.

While several species of seals and sea lions are shrinking, the California sea lion population is steadily on the rise. Their current world population is estimated between two and three hundred thousand. Although their population is rising, they are also commonly found in need of medical attention in the water and along the California coast. Sea lions commonly get caught up in fishing nets and suffer from malnutrition as a direct result. Like humans, sea lions have also been known to contract cancer. Yearlings (juvenile sea lions) can also suffer malnutrition as a result of early separation from their mothers and need medical intervention in order to achieve maximum health. Sea lions have also been known to suffer from domoic acid toxicosis which is caused by algal blooms in the ocean, leading to seizures.

19. Canadian Geese

Canadian Geese are a species of geese, distinctive by a black neck and head, a brown body and white splotches on the face. These birds are native to cooler climates of North America, although they've been found to migrate as far away as Europe. Branta Canadesis was popularly described in Sytema Naturae by Carl Linnaeus, although its first reference dates back to 1772.

The Branta genus predominately describes geese whose feathers are mostly black, separating them from the grey-colored plumage of the Anser genus. The Canada goose has a distinctive trait that differentiates it from all other species of geese world-wide. It has a white "chin strap" that is distinctive on it's black neck and head. The Barnacle goose also has a chinstrap, but it's chest is black and grey plumage on the body.

Canadian geese have several different subspecies making up the genus as a whole which vary in size and coloration, but these seven subspecies are all distinctly Canadian geese. Canadian geese can be anywhere between 30 and 43 inches long, and it's wingspan frequently ranges between 50-73 inches. Males and females are roughly the same size, but males weigh slightly more than their female counterparts and often display aggressive tendencies when defending their territory and breeding ground. Male and female Canadian geese are virtually indistinguishable in coloration and plumage, yet they make different sounding vocalizations.

Canadian geese often breed and are found in the Northern United States, and there is a large population to be found around the Great Lakes in particular. Canadian geese that make their home on the Pacific Coast as well as the Eastern seaboard often stay there year-round as the temperature fluctuations are more moderate than in more northern climates. Canadian geese often migrate to California, South Carolina and even Mexico in the winter months.

Canadian geese were over-hunted between the 19th and early 20th century, and as a result their numbers significantly dwindled. In fact, a large number of researchers believed the Giant Canada Goose was extinct for a time until a small population was discovered in Minnesota. Breeding facilities began monitoring these birds and their populations, and they began successfully breeding pairs to ensure their survival. over 6,000 giant Canadian Geese have been bred and released into the wild.

Restricted hunting opportunities and stricter hunting laws have allowed the population of Canadian geese in the north to replenish itself, and in many areas populations have thoroughly recovered their numbers.

Read More Amazing Animal Books
Website http://AmazingAnimalBooks.com

**Join our newsletter and receive
Amazing Animal Fact Sheets and
Get new books to review as soon as they come out**

This book is published by

**JD-Biz Corp
P O Box 374
Mendon, Utah 84325**
http://www.jd-biz.com/

Read more books from John Davidson

Over 500 Books and over 500,000 copies Downloaded

Made in United States
Troutdale, OR
10/04/2024

23415987R00038